HTML5 and CSS3

The Basics
Introduction for Beginners

Table of Contents

Introduction

The need for websites is on the rise. Companies, institutions and organizations are in need of website through which they can provide their potential customers with information of who they are. Websites are also a good way of communicating with clients. It is now possible for you to purchase items through websites, and the items will be shipped to your destination. All this is done without the need for your physical presence where the product is being sold. HTML5 and CSS3 are good programming languages for development of websites. These two have introduced new features that you can use to develop attractive websites and web applications. This book guides you on how to use HTML5 and CSS3 for web development. Enjoy reading!

Chapter 1- Getting Started

Html5 and Css3 are the latest versions of both Html and CSS. They have brought in new features that were not available in the older versions of the same.

Html5 has the following DOCTYPE declaration:

<!DOCTYPE html>

The character encoding declaration (charset) is also simple as shown below:

<meta charset="UTF-8">

Consider the HTML5 code given below:

```
<!DOCTYPE html>
<html>
<head>
<meta charset="UTF-8">
<title>Title of your document</title>
</head>
<body>
Content of your document......
</body>

</html>
```

That is the template that should be used when writing Html5 code. In HTML5, the UTF-8, is used as the default character encoding.

HTML5 is supported in all the latest versions of Apple Safari, Google Chrome, Mozilla Firefox, and Opera browsers.

To get started with HTML5 and CSS3, you should only have a basic text editor such as Notepad and a web browser such as Mozilla Firefox.

Chapter 2- HTML5 Basics

Attributes

Attributes are used for setting for setting the properties of an element. Some attributes are specific to an element while others are global. Each attributed should be given a name and a value.

Here is an attribute that shows how you can mark a div element:

<div class="sample">...</div>

The attribute has been given the name *sample.* The attribute should be specified in a start tag but not in an end tag. Note that the HTML5 attributes are not cases sensitive; hence you may write them in uppercase, lowercase or a mixture of the two. However, the common convention is that you stick to lowercase.

Below are the attributes that are supported by all the HTML5 tags:

- Access key - used to specify a keyboard element that can be used to access an element.

- Align - this can help in aligning an element horizontally. It can take right, center or left as the values.

- Background - this helps in specifying a background image to an element. It takes the URL to the background image.

- Bgcolor - this is used for specifying a background color behind an element.

- Class - this is for classifying an element so that it can be used with cascading style sheets.

- Contenteditable - for specifying whether a user will be allowed to edit the contents of an element or not.

- Contextmenu - for specifying the context menu of an element. Takes the menu id as the value.

- Draggable - for specifying whether users will be allowed to drag the element or not.

- Height - used for specifying the height of table cells, images or tables.

- Tabindex - for specifying the tab order of an element.
- Subject- for specifying the corresponding item of an element.

- Valign - for aligning tags vertically with an element.

Above are just some of the tags supported in HTML5.

HTML5 has also introduced a new feature known as *Custom Data Attributes*. The custom data attribute should begin with *data* depending on your requirement. Consider the example given below:

<div class="sample" data-subject="chemistry" data-level="complex">

...
</div>

We have created two custom attributes named *data-subject* and *data-level*.

Headings

To define headings, we use the <h1> to <h6> tags, with the <h1> tag denoting the most important heading in the document. Example:

<h1>This is H1-heading</h1>
<h3>This is H3-heading</h3>
<h6>This is H6-heading</h4>

Headings are of great importance as they give your web pages a structure. Ensure that you use them when you need to create headings rather than when you need to write your text in bold. Consider the HTML code that uses headings to give a structure to your page:

```
<!DOCTYPE html>
<html>
<head>
    <title>A HTML5 Document</title>
</head>
<body>
    <h1>Introduction</h1>
        <p>This is  paragraph in a HTML document</p>
    <h2>This is a less important heading</h2>
        <p>This is our second paragraph below h2-heading</p>
    <h3>A 3rd level heading</h3>
        <p> A new paragraph  </p>
    <h2> 2nd level headings</h2>
    <h2>Our last 2nd level heading</h2>
</body>
</html>
```

The above code gives the following structure:

Classes and Id's

Id's and class attributes help you in changing and enhancing the structure of your web pages.

ID

This is an attribute used to give a name to your element. The name of the element must be unique and it should not be used anywhere else within that document. The id is simply an abbreviation for identifier, and it should be used anytime that you want to be able to identify the element uniquely. You can use the HTML markup with Id element to identify the columns:
<div id="right-column">Right column content</div>

<div id="left-column"> Left column content</div>

Note that each element should be given a unique ID.

Classes

These are used for assigning general properties to an element. This is an indication that you can have several elements using one class name. This is because you may want all of these elements to behave in a similar manner. Example:

<div class="blog-part">
    **<p> Another Day
**
    **Written by Nicholas
**
    On January 28th </p>
    <p class="content"> My second blog entry, just testing how it works. </p>

```
</div>
<div class="blog-part">
    <p> First Blog Entry <br />
    Written by Nicholas<br />
    On January 28th </p>
    <p class="content">Feeling excited today! I must
enjoy the day!</p>
<div>
```
Links

A link is simply a word, a group of words, or an image that one clicks to open a new document or move to another part within the same document. In HTML5, links are added using the <a> tag, which is an abbreviation for anchor. You can then use href which is an abbreviation for hypertext reference to add the address or url you are linking to. Example:

```
<a href="http://www.url.com">Link text</a>
```

Sometimes, you may need the link to open in a new window once the text is clicked. This can be done using the *target* attribute. Example:

```
<a href="http://www.url.com" target="_blank">A
link</a>
```

When user clicks the text in the above example, the link will be opened in a new link.

There are two ways for you to link it to a part of the document. Previously, you could give that place a name then use it to create the link as follows:

<a name="part2">This</a> answers the question in part 2.

It is known as a fragment identifier as it is used to identify a specific fragment of the document. You can also use an anchor identifier as shown below:

<a href="#part2">Here is the answer to question in part 2</a>

An id can be used as follows:

<p id="a-note">A section having unique id.</p>
<p>This is a section without id or anything else</p>
<a href="#a-note">Move to first section</a>

If the first paragraph element had no id and but we are still in need of linking to first section, we could have done it as follows:

<p><a name="a-note" />The first section having a unique id</p>

<p>This is a section without id's or anything else</p>
<a href="#a-note">Move to first section</a>

Images

To define images in HTML, we use the <img> tag. This tag has only attributes with no closing tag. The easiest way for you to use this tag is via the src attribute, that is, source attribute. The value of this attribute should be the URL for the image that you want to display. The URL should point to where you have stored your image which is mostly in your server as shown below:

<img src="picture.jpg">

Other than the src attribute, you are also required to set the *alt* attribute. This is an abbreviation for alternate text. This is what should be shown in case the browser is not capable of showing the image. The readers will also see the text below the image. Use this to describe your image. Example:

<img src="picture.jpg" alt="Portrait of Nicholas">

Lists

Lists have a number of uses in web development. You can use them to show the contents of a recipe as well as table of contents for a particular document.
HTML supports two types of lists, that is, ordered and unordered lists.

The unordered list is denoted using the <ul> tag for unordered list, while the ordered list is denoted by the <li> tag for list item. This is shown below:

```
<ul>
    <li>List item 1</li>
    <li>List item 2</li>
    <li>List item 3</li>
</ul>
```

In unordered list, black circles are used as the bullet points. However, you can use CSS to change how these bullet points appear.

Items in an ordered list are marked with numbers. We use the <ol> tag to create an ordered list rather than the <ul> tag as shown below:

```
<ol>
    <li>List item 1</li>
    <li>List item 2</li>
    <li>List item 3</li>
</ol>
```

Most web designers use lists when they are creating menus for their websites as well as navigations.
This is because the navigation is made of a set of related links. CSS is then used to style them and in case it fails, the links will still have a structure.

Text Formatting

You should not use HTML for styling your web content, but this should be done with CSS. In the previous versions of HTML, the <li>, <b> and <em> tags were solely used for styling text, but new semantics have been added to them in HTML5:

- The <i> tag was for writing text in italics, but now it is used for alternate text like technical terms, foreign words and online stage directions.

- The <b> tag was used for writing text in bold, now it can also be used for stylistic offset like keywords in some document having product names.

- The <em> tag was used for putting emphasis; it can now be used for words and sentences that are to be pronounced differently.

- The <strong> tag is used for denoting something with a strong emphasis, it shows importance.

The following example demonstrates how these tags can be used:

**This is a foreign word, <i>tuko</i>, means present in Swahili

**

**The phrase <b>I am</b> shows one's confidence in himself

**

**Alternate? Use <em>em</em>, instead of the italic element.

**

For you to write a semantic code <strong>ensure that you know the differences</strong>!

Blockquotes

The <blockquote> tag is used for marking website content that has been copied from some other website. It should be used as shown below:

17

```html
<article>
<header>
    <h1>All About Dogs</h1>
    <p class="byline">by Nicholas</p>
</header>
<section>
    <h2>The Types of Dogs</h2>
    <p>There are various ...</p>
    <p>Feed your dog well and it will ...</p>
</section>
<blockquote>
Here, add the text that you have copied from another
website. We will then use the tag to designate that it
has been copied from another website. <br />

    Jonh  Joel, <a
href="http://www.johnjoel.com">johnjoel.com</a>
</blockquote>

<section>... </section>
</article>
```

Chapter 3- Web Forms 2.0

The web forms 2.0 are an extension of the forms features that are found in HTML4. In HTML5, these features have been enhanced so that the work of the programmer is made easy. One does not have to do much scripting as it was in HTML4.

The <input> element

In HTML4, the input elements make use of the *type* attribute to specify the data type for the element. HTML has various types including text, password, checkbox, radio, submit, file, image, hidden, select, text area and button. The inputs are defined using the <input> tag:

```
<input type="text" />
<input />
```

Consider the simple example given below:
...

```
<form action="send.php" method="post">

  <p>

    <label for="firstname">First Name: </label>
    <input type="text" id="firstname"><br />
<label for="lastname">Last Name: </label>
    <input type="text" id="lastname"><br />

    <label for="email">Email: </label>
    <input type="text" id="email"><br>

    <input type="radio" name="sex" value="male">
Male<br>
```

```
<input type="radio" name="sex" value="female">
Female<br>
<input type="submit" value="send"> <input
type="reset">

</p>
</form>
```
...

For the case of HTML5, new values have been introduced for the *type* attribute. Creating forms in HTML5, we use the *<form>* tag.

datetime

This creates a text field in which a user can enter the date value. Example:

```
<form action = "send.php" method = "get">
Date and Time : <input type = "datetime" name =
"newinput" />
<input type = "submit" value = "submit" />
</form>
```

The *action* field specifies the name of the file that will be called once the user clicks the *Submit* button.

Time

This allows the user to create a field for time and it is encoded according to ISO 8601. Example:

```
<form action = "send.php" method = "get">
Time : <input type = "time" name = "newinput" />
```

```
<input type = "submit" value = "submit" />
</form>
```
Number

This helps you create a field that will accept only numerical values. You can use the *step* attribute in order to specify the precision, with its default being 1. Example:

```
<form action = "file.php" method = "get">
    Select Number : <input type = "number" min =
"0" max = "10" step "1"
    value = "5" name = "newinput" />
  <input type = "submit" value = "submit" />
</form>
```
email

This is used to create a field that will only accept an email value. In case you submit a value that is not an email address, you will be forced to enter an email address. It is created as follows:

```
<form action = "file.php" method = "get">
  Enter email : <input type = "email" name =
"newinput" />
  <input type = "submit" value = "submit" />
</form>
```
url

This helps you create a field that will only accept a URL value. If you submit a simple text, you will be forced to enter a URL. The url should be in **http://www.name.com** or **http://name.com** format. Example:

```
<form action = "file.php" method = "get">
```

Enter URL : <input type = "url" name = "newinput" />
  <input type = "submit" value = "submit" />
</form>

Grouping Form Elements

Sometimes, you may have a lengthy form, requiring you to group the various elements together. This can be done using the <fieldset> tag. The group name is given by first <legend> element, which is simply a child of <childset> element. You can use the <label> tag to add a caption if you need.

Consider the example given below:

```
<form>
    <fieldset>
        <legend>Contact Details</legend>
            <label for="name">Name:</label>
            <input id="name"><br />

            <label for="telephone">Telephone:</label>
            <input id="telephone"><br />

            <label for="email">Email:</label>
            <input id="email">
    </fieldset>
    <fieldset>
        <legend>About User</legend>
            <label for="username">Username:</label>
            <input id="username"><br />
```

```
            <label
for="password">Password:</label>
            <input id="password"><br />
    </fieldset>
    <input type="submit" value="Submit now" />
</form>
```

Sending Form Data

Once you have entered data into a form, you have the choice of sending it to a database, to your email or to another web page. You can choose the one you need and define the way in which the browser handles the user input. The definition of this is done via a method attribute, which takes either *get* or *post*:

```
<form action="url" method="post">
```

When you use *get*, the data will be encoded by browser into URL while when you use *post*, the data will be sending to an email or database.

The easiest way for sending data is sending it to an email address. You only have to add action element to your form element as well as the method attribute. The action attribute is responsible for telling your browser on what to do with your form contents while the method attribute tells the browser how to handle the data. Example:

```
<form action="mailto:your@email.com"
method="post">
    First name: <input type="text"
name="firstname" />
    Surname: <input type="text" name="surname"
/>
```

23

```
    <input type="submit" value="Submit now" />
</form>
```

Once you use the above method, the functionality will be determined by the email client that you have installed on your computer. This is an indication that not all the users will be in a position to use your form.

Multiline Textboxes

In some cases, you may need the user to type in a number of lies in a field. This is a good circumstance for you to use the <textarea> tag. You can use the *rows* and *cols* attributes for changing the size of the text area. Example:

```
<form method="post">
    <textarea cols="20" rows="7"></textarea>
    <br />
    <input type="submit" value="Submit now" />
</form>
```

In the above example, I have created a text area with 20 rows and 7 columns.

Radiobuttons

This is a good option for you when you need to present a number of choices to the user while expecting the user to select only one of them. To group radio buttons, a set of radio buttons is given one name to form a group, and the user is only allowed to choose one radiobutton within a group. The *value* attribute helps in specifying the value that will be sent to your email.

Example:

<input type="radio" name="your-group" value="unit-in-group" />Unit-in-group

The following examples demonstrate how you can force a user to choose only one option in a group of radio buttons:

```
<form method="post">
    <fieldset>
        <legend>Choose Your Best Pet</legend>

        <input type="radio" name="animal" value="Cat" />Cats<br />

        <input type="radio" name="animal" value="Bird" />Birds<br />

        <input type="radio" name="animal" value="Dog" />Dogs<br />

        <input type="submit" value="Submit now" />
    </fieldset>
</form>
```

Checkboxes

This is a good alternative when you need to provide the user with a way of choosing many options within the group of choices.

The *type* attribute should take the value *checkbox* and all checkboxes within the same group should be given the same name. The value for *value* attribute will be the name to be sending to the email or database. Example:

<input type="checkbox" name="your-group" value="unit-in-group" />Unit-in-group

Checkboxes are a good way of presenting options to users when you need them to be able to choose more than one options within a group. Example:

```
<form method="post">
    <fieldset>
      <legend>Choose Your Best Pet</legend>

        <input type="checkbox" name="animal"
value="Cat" />Cats <br />

         <input type="checkbox" name="animal"
value="Dog" />Dogs<br />

        <input type="checkbox" name="animal"
value="Bird" />Birds<br />

        <input type="submit" value="Submit now" />
    </fieldset>
</form>
```

Submit and Reset Buttons

To create buttons, we change the type attribute of the input element. There are two types of buttons that is the reset and submit buttons.

You should use a submit button when you are submitting the contents of a form. It has the following markup:

<input type="submit" value="Submit Form" />

The reset button helps you reset all the input fields of a form. It has the following markup:

<input type="reset" value="Reset" />

Here is how you can create a simple form featuring both submit and reset buttons:

**<form action="mailto:name@domain.com"
method="post">**

**First name: <input type="text"
name="firstname" />
**
**Surname: <input type="text" name="surname"
/>
**

<input type="reset" value="Clear form" />
<input type="submit" value="Submit Form" />
</form>

You can press the reset button anytime that you want to clear the form fields, but the submit button should be pressed the last one since it will initiate the submission of the form details.

Dropdown Lists

This is one of the ways through which you can prompt a user to choose only one option from a series of options. The first choice in the dropdown list forms the default choice. This makes it ideal for use when you know the choice that is highly preferred by users. Note that you must choose an item from the dropdown list as it is not optional for the user to select one option from the list.

To create a dropdown list, we use the <select> tag and the values in the list are specified via the *value* tag. Example:

```
<form method="post">
    <select name="Available Icecream Flavours">
        <option value="vanilla">Vanilla</option>
        <option value="double chocolate">Double
Chocolate</option>

        <option value="caramel">Caramel</option>
        <option
value="strawberry">Strawberry</option>

    </select>
</form>
```

If you need another item to act as the default other than the first one, you should use the *selected* attribute. HTML5 has made this simple, so instead of having to write:

```
<option value="caramel"
selected="selected">Caramel</option>
```

You can write:

```
<form>
    <select name="Available Icecream Flavours">
        <option value="vanilla">Vanilla</option>
        <option value="double chocolate">Double
Chocolate</option>

        <option value="caramel">Caramel</option>
        <option value="strawberry"
selected>Strawberry</option>


    </select>
</form>
```

Chapter 4- Tables

Tables are normally used for the purpose of displaying data to the users. In some cases, tables are used for dividing the web pages but avoid this as they are less flexible compared to the divs.

Table is created using the <table> tag. It should be the first element in a table and it states that the other markups will be inside a table. Tables are structured using rows and columns. However, columns have no tags unlike rows. Each row is created using the <tr> tag for table row, while each cell is created using the <td> data which means table data. You must define the structure of your table before beginning to create it as this will make it easy for you to create it. The following is an example of a simple table:

```
<table border="1" width="100%">
        <tr>
                <td>Cell 1 at Row 1</td>
                <td>Cell 2 at Row 1</td>
                <td>Cell 3 at Row 2</td>
        </tr>
        <tr>
                <td>Cell 1 at Row 2</td>
                <td>Cell 2 at Row 2</td>
                <td>Cell 3 at Row 2</td>
```

```
     </tr>
          <tr>
               <td>Cell 1 at Row 3</td>
               <td>Cell 2 at Row 3</td>
               <td>Cell 3 at Row 3</td>
          </tr>
          <tr>
               <td>Cell 1 at Row 4</td>
               <td>Cell 2 at Row 4</td>
               <td>Cell 3 at Row 4</td>
          </tr>
     </table>
```

Cell 1 at Row 1	Cell 2 at Row 1	Cell 3 at Row 2
Cell 1 at Row 2	Cell 2 at Row 2	Cell 3 at Row 2
Cell 1 at Row 3	Cell 2 at Row 3	Cell 3 at Row 3
Cell 1 at Row 4	Cell 2 at Row 4	Cell 3 at Row 4

As you have seen in the above table, each <td> tag is inside a <tr> tag. All the <td> tags inside one <tr> tag will be added to the same row.

Colspan and Rowspan

HTML markup has been designed in such a way that you can add different number of cells into a row. In some rows, you can have four cells, three cells in others etc.
For you to achieve this you must use the colspan and rowspan attributes. These attributes normally take a whole number as the value.

Let us use our previous example but make the first row to have two cells rather than three. We will also be merging and second cell of rows three and four:

```
<table border="1" width="100%">
    <tr>
        <td colspan="2">Cell 1 at Row 1</td>
            <td>Cell 2 at Row 1</td>

        </tr>
        <tr>
            <td>Cell 1 at Row 2</td>
            <td>Cell 2 at Row 2</td>
            <td>Cell 3 at Row 2</td>
        </tr>
        <tr>
            <td>Cell 1 at Row 3</td>
          <td rowspan="2">Cell 2 at Row 3</td>
            <td>Cell 3 at Row 3</td>
        </tr>
        <tr>
            <td>Cell 1 at Row 4</td>
            <td>Cell 3 at Row 4</td>
        </tr>
</table>
```

This gives the following table:

Cell 1 at Row 1		Cell 2 at Row 1
Cell 1 at Row 2	Cell 2 at Row 2	Cell 3 at Row 2
Cell 1 at Row 3	Cell 2 at Row 3	Cell 3 at Row 3
Cell 1 at Row 4		Cell 3 at Row 4

In the first row, we have used the colspan attribute so that the first cell can occupy two columns. In the third row, we have used the rowspan attribute so that the second row spans two rows. The cell that is occupied after spanning the columns or the rows has been removed.

Thead and Tbody

You might be in need of having a table that is structured very well. This calls for you to advance your table further. This can be done using these two elements. The <thead> tag helps in creating headings for your table. The <tbody> tag helps in structuring the contents of the table, after which the browser will be able to tell the actual content of the table. We can add these elements to our previous example as follows:

```
<table border="1" width="100%">
<thead>
    <tr>
            <td>Cell 1 at Row 1</td>
            <td>Cell 2 at Row 1</td>
            <td>Cell 3 at Row 2</td>
        </tr>
</thead>
<tbody>
        <tr>
            <td>Cell 1 at Row 2</td>
            <td>Cell 2 at Row 2</td>
            <td>Cell 3 at Row 2</td>
        </tr>
        <tr>
            <td>Cell 1 at Row 3</td>
            <td>Cell 2 at Row 3</td>
            <td>Cell 3 at Row 3</td>
```

```
        </tr>
        <tr>
            <td>Cell 1 at Row 4</td>
            <td>Cell 2 at Row 4</td>
            <td>Cell 3 at Row 4</td>
        </tr>
</tbody>
</table>
```

However, to creating the heading for the table, you should use the <th> tag.

The following example demonstrates how you can use the <th> tag:

```
<table border="1" width="100%">
    <thead>
        <tr>
            <th>Name</th>
            <th>AGe</th>
            <th>Weight</th>
        </tr>
    </thead>
    <tbody>
        <tr>
            <th>John</th>
            <td>25</td>
            <td>55</td>
        </tr>
        <tr>
            <th>Nicholas</th>
            <td>26</td>
            <td>77</td>
        </tr>
        <tr>
```

```
        <th>Lilian</th>
        <td>24</td>
        <td>58</td>
    </tr>
  </tbody>
</table>
```

Other than the <th> tag, you can use CSS to style your table.

Changing Column Width

You can use percentages to alter the width of your table columns. The width of all columns in a row should add up to 100%. This can be done using the *col* attribute as shown below:

```
<table border="1" width="100%">
    <col style="width:40%">
    <col style="width:30%">
    <col style="width:30%">
    <thead>
    <tr>
        <th>Fruits</th>
        <th>Vitamin A</th>
        <th>Vitamin C</th>
    </tr>
    </thead>
    <tbody>
    <tr>
                <th>John</th>
        <td>25</td>
        <td>55</td>
    </tr>
    <tr>
        <th>Nicholas</th>
```

```
        <td>26</td>
        <td>77</td>
    </tr>
    <tr>
        <th>Lilian</th>
        <td>24</td>
        <td>58</td>
    </tr>
  </tbody>
</table>
```

That is how you can control the width of your table.

Chapter 5- HTML5 Tags

HTML5 has numerous tags that are used to group sections of the web pages. Let us discuss them.

The article Tag

This tag has been introduced in HTML5 and it can be used to place some emphasis on a section of content. However, this tag should not be used whenever you are writing a paragraph. It is denoted as <article>. Example:

```
<article>
    <div id="header">
        <h1>About Dog</h1>
        ...
    </div>
    <div id="content">
        <h2>The Types of Dogs</h2>
            <p>These      are      the      types      of
dogs....</p>
            <h2>Dog Characteristics</h2>
            <p>All dogs are...</p>
        ...
    </div>
</article>
```

The header Tag

This is used to create a heading for an already existing section, but not for introducing a new section. Avoid confusing it with the <head> element. It is created as follows:

<header>...</header>

The following example demonstrates how you can use this tag:

```
<article>
    <header>
        <h1>About Dogs</h1>
        <p class="teaser">Dogs are good for home
security.</p>
        <p class="byline">by Nicholas</p>
    </header>

    <div id="content">
        <h2>The Types of Dogs</h2>
```

Whenever you are using the <header> tag, ensure that you have at least one heading tag, that is, h1 to h6.

The footer Tag

You regularly see footers on the websites that you visit. It should be used as the part of a particular section as opposed to introducing a new section. This makes it possible for you to have multiple footers on a website. It is created using the <footer> tag as demonstrated below:

```
</header>
<div id="content">
    <h2>Types of Dogs</h2>
    ...
</div>
<footer>
    <p class="disclaimer">This article is copyright of mysite.com</p>

    <p><a href="http://mysite.com/howto/all-about-dogs/">See the original article here</a></p>

    <p>Part of <a href="http://www.mysite-tutorials.org">Mysite-tutorials.org</a></p>

</footer>
</article>
```

If the footer tag has nothing else other than links, create it as shown below:

```
<footer>
    <ul>
        <li>About us</li>
        <li>Contact us</li>
        </ul>
</footer>
```

The navigation Tag

The <nav> tag is a new element in HTML5. It is a representation of navigation for a document. This can be within the document or in the other documents but note that not all the links contained in a document should be marked with the <nav> tag.

In the early days of HTML, you could only use the <div> as shown below:

```
<div id="menu">
    <ul>
        <li><a href="about.html">About us</a></li>
        ...
    </ul>
</div>
```

Or something related to the following:

```
<div id="navigation">
    <ul>
        <li><a href="about.html">About us</a></li>
        ...
    </ul>
</div>
```

In HTML5, you are only required to replace the old <div> with <nav> as shown below:

```
<nav>
    <ul>
        <li><a href="about.html">About us</a></li>
        ...
    </ul>
</nav>
```

This shows that you can use the <nav> tag where you could have used the <div> tag.

The section Tag

This is one of the hard tags for one to learn how to use. Compared to the <article> tag, it is a bit general, but you should have an actual section when using the <section> tag. You can use the <section> tag to divide different parts of an article as shown below:

```
</header>
<section>
    <h2> Types of Dogs</h2>
    <p>There are various ...</p>
</section>

<section>
    <h2>First Dog Type</h2>
    <p>This is a ... </p>
</section>
...
<footer>...</footer>
</article>
```

41

Several markup lines are added to the document but most of them prefer a very little markup. You are not required to use the <section> tag in your article but it gives it a nice outline when used.

The aside Tag

The <aside> is a new tag introduced in HTML5. Its context is determined by whether it is inside or outside the article element. When reading magazines, you normally see some content that has been pulled from the main article and written aside.
Its content is related to what is contained in the main article. The following example demonstrates how the <aside> element can be placed inside the <article> element:

```
<article>
    <header>
        <h1>About Dogs<h1>
        <p class="byline">by Nicholas</p>
    </header>
    <section>
        <h2>The Types of Dogs</h2>
        <p>There are various type ...</p>
        <p>With the difference being brought by
...</p>
    </section>
    <aside>
        If you treat your dog well, it will always
remain active.
    </aside>
</article>
```

You can also use the <aside> tag to mark some content that is very relevant to the entire page. Example:

```
<aside>
    <h3>The websites I like</h3>
    <a href="http://www.site1.com">Site 1</a>
    <a href="http://site2.com/"> Site 2</a>
    <a href="http://www.site3.com">Site 3</a>
</aside>
<article>

    <section>
            <h2>The Types of Dogs</h2>
        <p>There are various type ...</p>
        <p>With the difference being brought by ...</p>
    </section>
    </p>
</article>
```

Always note that the <aside> tag should only be used for secondary content.

The address Tag

This is a new tag in HTML5. It should be related to the element in which it has been nested. The following example demonstrates how the <address> tag can be used:

```
<article>
<header>
    <hgroup>
    <h1>About Dogs<h1>
```

43

\<h2\> If you treat your dog well, it will always remain active.\</h2\>

\</hgroup\>
\<address\>by Nicholas\</address\>
\</header\>

You can use the \<address\> tag to show the authors of sections. Example:

\<article\>
\<header\>
    \<h1\>About Dogs\<h1\>
    \<p class="byline"\>by Nicholas\</p\>
\</header\>
\<section\>
    \<h2\>The are various Types of...\</h2\>
    \<p\>What you should know is...\</p\>
    \<p\>Feed it well and see ...\</p\>
\</section\>
\<blockquote\>

    This is a new tag in HTML5. It should be related to the element in which it has been nested. \<br /\>
    \<address\>Nicholas, www.mysite.com\</address\>
\</blockquote\>
\</article\>

Chapter 6- Form Validation

After creating a web form to collect information from the visitors, you will find that some visitors will get confused when filling out the form. It is good for you to validate the form in order to ensure that the visitors provide the right details. A good example of a field is the email address field. If you need to contact your visitors via email, you will ask them to provide their email addresses. You need to ensure that the visitors provide a valid email address; otherwise, you will not be able to contact them.

The following is an example shows an un-validated form:

```
<form>
    <input type="text" required="required" /><br />
    <input type="submit" value="Submit Form" />
</form>
```

The required Attribute

The *required* attribute is used when you have a text field that you don't the user to leave it blank. This is an easy way of validation as opposed to what one had to do before HTML5. It can be used as shown below:

```
<form>
    <input type="text" required="required" /><br />
    <input type="submit" value="Submit Form" />
</form>
```

You can also write it in a short way as shown below:

45

```
<form>
    <input type="text" required /><br />
    <input type="submit" value="Submit Form" />
</form>
```

Validation of Email Addresses

When you need to prompt users to enter an email address, you must create an input of type *email*. The browser will know that the user is expected to enter an email address, so it will ensure that the entered value is a valid email address:

```
<input type="email" />
```

Note that the type in the above case has been set as *email*. When this is done, the browser will expect a user to type a valid email address. Here is a simple form that requires the user to enter an email address:

```
<form>
    <input type="email" required /> <br />
    <input type="submit" value="Submit Form">
</form>
```

For some browsers, only the @ symbol will be looked at. For other browsers, the dot that follows the @ symbol will be checked.

You can also use a pattern to value the field for the email address. Consider the example given below:

```
<form>
    <input pattern="/^[a-zA-Z0-
9.!#$%&'*+/=?^_`{|}~-]+@[a-zA-Z0-9-]+(?:\.[a-zA-
Z0-9-]+)*$/" required />
    <br />
    <input type="submit" value="Submit Form">
</form>
```

With the above pattern, the browser will check whether you have entered a valid email address. The email address must consist with a dot and @ symbol.

Validating URLs

URLs may differ in terms of structure. Note that it is not a must for a URL to include a dot (.). Also, a URL should not include a space. You can use the *url* type for the tag to require users to enter a url address:

```
<input type="url" />
```

To require that users must type something in the URL field, you can add the *required* attribute as shown below:

```
<form>
    <input type="url" required />
    <input type="submit" value="Submit Form">
</form>
```

To enhance validation of the URL field, we can add a search pattern to the input field. We should use the JavaScript Regular expressions in order to create the search pattern. The pattern should be of the form *pattern="https?://.+"* and you will have improved the URL validation. This is shown below:

```
<form>
    <input type="url" pattern="https?://.+" required
/>
    <input type="submit" value="Submit Form">
</form>
```
Validating Phone Numbers

This is another input that browsers do not support. There is no pattern for phone numbers that browsers should follow or check like for email and URLs. One of the reasons behind this is that there is no standard form of writing phone numbers as they differ from one country to another. However, whenever you want users to type in a phone number, ensure that you use the input type of *tel* so that the input may checked to be semantically correct. This is shown below:

```
<form>
    Phone Number: <input type="tel" required />
    <input type="submit" value="Submit Form" />
</form>
```

The good thing with this input type is that when typing the value in it, the keyboard will be changed from the regular QWERTY keyboard to a number pad. This has an effect of improving the user experience.

Validating Dates

HTML5 provides you with a way of validating dates. In some browsers, the user will be provided with a drop down from which they can pick the date. This way, the users will not be confused about the format of the date to use. They will also not give wrong or non-existent dates. To require an input of date with month, year and date, use the *date* input type as follows:

```
<form>
 <input type="date">
 <input type="submit" value="Submit Form">
</form>
```

To require a user to enter a month, validate it by using the *month* input type as follows:

```
<form>
 <input type="month">
 <input type="submit" value="Submit Form">
</form>
```

For the case of a week, use the *week* input type as follows:

```
<form>
 <input type="week">
 <input type="submit" value="Submit Form">
</form>
```

When you require users to enter a time, use the *time* input type which is of the form HH:mm:ss.ss with the seconds being optional. This is shown below:

```
<form>
 <input type="time">
 <input type="submit" value="Submit Form">
</form>
```

To require both date and time from the users, use the *datetime* input type as shown below:

```
<form>
 <input type="datetime">
 <input type="submit" value="Submit Form">
</form>
```

Placeholder

A placeholder helps in guiding a user on the kind of data they are expected to enter in a particular text
field. If you want to enter a phone number for example, and you need it to start with the country code, you can use a placeholder to instruct or guide the user to do so. This is shown below:

```
<form>
    First Name: <input type="text"
name="firstname" placeholder="example, Mercy"/>
<br>

Phone: <input type="tel" name="phone"
placeholder="example, +254725626821"/> <br>

<input type="submit" value="Submit Form" />
</form>
```

Chapter 7- Linking CSS to HTML

CSS stands for Cascading Style Sheet. It is used for styling HT<ML documents and web pages. Just like any other programming language, you can create the *hello world* code for CSS. This is demonstrated below:

```
<style type="text/css">
h1 {
     color: DeepSkyBlue;
}
</style>
```

```
<h1>Hello, World</h1>
```

The above will print the "Hello, World" text with the specified color, that is, DeepSkyBlue. What we have done is that we have created a text with <h1> tag, and then we have created a rule that was to change the color of the text. Here is the rule targeted to the h1 elements of the code:

```
h1 {
     color: DeepSkyBlue;
}
```

To note that the rule is targeted for h1 elements, we must place the h1 outside the curly brace as shown
 above. Note that we have used a colon (:) to separate the rule name from the value, and the entire rule ends with a semicolon (;). Consider a more complex example given below:

```
h1, h2, h3 {
     color: DeepSkyBlue;
     background-color: #000;
```

```
    margin: 10px 5px;
}

h2 {
    color: GreenYellow;
}
```

Whenever you want to link HTML and CSS, you can do it directly from the HTML code. The best way to do this is via a style block. HTML has a tag known as style which can have a CSS code. Consider the example given below:

```
<!DOCTYPE html>
<html>
<head>
    <title>Style</title>
    <style type="text/css">
    .highlight {
        color: Blue;
        text-decoration: underline;
    }
    </style>
</head>
<body>

This is some<span class="highlight">text</span>
having <span class="highlight">highlighted</span>
some elements in <span class="highlight">it</span>.

</body>
</html>
```

You can also create two different files, one with HTML code and the other with CSS code. The file with HTML5 code should end with .html extension while the one for CSS should end with .css extension. Here is the code for a file named *style.css*:

```
.highlight {
    color: Blue;
    text-decoration: underline;
}
```

We can then reference the above file in our HTML document so that the two can be linked together. This is shown below:

```
<!DOCTYPE html>
<html>
<head>
    <title>Styles</title>
    <link rel="stylesheet" type="text/css" href="style.css" />
</head>
<body>

This is some<span class="highlight">text</span> having <span class="highlight">highlighted</span> some elements in <span class="highlight">it</span>.

</body>
</html>
```

Chapter 8- Setting Background Properties

There are various background properties that you can set via CSS. These properties include image, color, repeat, position, attachment etc.

Setting Background color

You can set the background color of an element via CSS. This can be done as follows:

```
<body>
  <p style = "background-color:blue;">
  This is text has a blue background color.</p>
</body>
```

Note that we have used the "background-color" attribute to set the background color of the element.

Setting Background Image

You can call some images that you stored locally and set them as the background image. This can be done as shown below:

```
<html>
  <head>
    <style>
      body {
        background-image: url("/css/images/img.jpg");
        background-color: #cccccc;
      }
    </style>
    <body>
      <h1>Hello, World</h1>
```

```
    </body>
   </head>
<html>
```

We have used the *background-image* property then we have passed the path leading to the image in the *url* attribute. It is a jpeg image named *img*.

Repeating Background Image

If the image is small, you may choose to repeat it in the background. This can be done using the *background-repeat* property, and if you don't the image to repeat itself, use the *no-repeat* property. This is demonstrated below:

```
<html>
  <head>
    <style>
      body {
        background-image: url("/css/images/img.jpg");
        background-repeat: repeat;
      }
    </style>
  </head>
  <body>
   <p>Hello, World</p>
  </body>
</html>
```

Note that the *background-repeat* property has been set to *repeat*, meaning that the image will be repeated in the background. To repeat the background image vertically, you set the property to *repeat-y* as shown below:

```
<html>
  <head>
    <style>
      body {
        background-image: url("/css/images/img.jpg");
        background-repeat: repeat-y;
      }
    </style>
  </head>
  <body>
    <p>Hello, World<//>
  </body>
</html>
```

To repeat the background image horizontally, use the *repeat-x* as the value of the attribute. This is shown below:

```
<html>
  <head>
    <style>
      body {
        background-image: url("/css/images/img.jpg");
        background-repeat: repeat-x;
      }
    </style>
  </head>
  <body>
    <p>Hello, World<//>
  </body>
</html>
```

Setting Position of Background Image

Sometimes, you may need to specify the position from the left or right at which to set the background image. This is possible using the *background-position* property as shown below:

```
<html>
  <head>
    <style>
      body {
        background-image: url("/css/images/img.jpg");
        background-position:110px;
      }
    </style>
  </head>
  <body>
    <p>Hello, World<//>
  </body>
</html>
```

The image will be set 110 pixels away from the left. You can specify the position to set the image from the left and down from the top as follows:

```
<html>
  <head>
    <style>
      body {
        background-image: url("/css/images/img.jpg");
        background-position:110px 180px;
      }
    </style>
  </head>
  <body>
    <p>Hello, World<//>
  </body>
```

</html>

The image will be set 110 pixels from the left and 180 pixels down from the top.

Gradients

With the CSS3 gradient feature, you can create a gradient from one color to another without the use of images. This is a good way of providing transitions between two or more colors. This was earlier done via images, but with gradients, you can reduce on download times and save on bandwidth.

Creating Linear Gradients

For you to create a linear gradient, you must define not less than two color stops. However, if you need to define complex gradient effects, you are expected to define more color stops. You may also set the starting point as well as the direction for the gradient. The following is the syntax for creating a gradient:

linear-gradient(direction, color-stop_1, color-stop_2, ...)

Top to Bottom

The following code can help you create a linear gradient from top to bottom:

```
<!DOCTYPE html>
<html lang="en">
<head>
<title>Top to Bottom Linear Gradients</title>
<style type="text/css">
        .gradient {
                width: 400px;
                height: 300px;
                /* A Fallback if the browser doesn't
support gradients */
                background: red;
                /* Safari 5.1 to 6.0 */
                background: -webkit-linear-
gradient(blue, yellow);
                /* Internet Explorer 10 */
                background: -ms-linear-gradient(blue,
yellow);
                /* Standard syntax */
                background: linear-gradient(blue,
yellow);
        }
</style>
</head>
<body>
  <div class="gradient"></div>
</body>
</html>
```

The output will be:

Left to Right

The following code can help you create a linear gradient from left to right:

```
<!DOCTYPE html>
<html lang="en">
<head>
<title>Left to Right Linear Gradients</title>
<style type="text/css">
        .gradient {
                width: 400px;
                height: 300px;
                /* A fallback if the browser doesn't
support gradients */
                background: red;
                /* Safari 5.1 to 6.0 */
                background: -webkit-linear-gradient(left,
blue, yellow);
                /* Internet Explorer 10 */
                background: -ms-linear-gradient(left,
blue, yellow);
                /* Standard syntax */
```

```
        background: linear-gradient(to right,
blue, yellow);
    }
</style>
</head>
<body>
  <div class="gradient"></div>
</body>
</html>
```

The output will be:

Diagonal

It is possible for you to create a gradient along the diagonal line. The following code will create one from the bottom left corner to the top right corner:

```
<!DOCTYPE html>
<html lang="en">
<head>
<title>Example of Linear Gradients along
Diagonal</title>
<style type="text/css">
    .gradient {
        width: 400px;
```

```
        height: 300px;
        /* A fallback if the browser doesn't
support gradients */
        background: red;
        /* Safari 5.1 to 6.0 */
        background: -webkit-linear-
gradient(bottom left, blue, yellow);
        /* Internet Explorer 10 */
        background: -ms-linear-gradient(bottom
left, blue, yellow);
        /* Standard syntax */
        background: linear-gradient(to top right,
blue, yellow);
    }
</style>
</head>
<body>
  <div class="gradient"></div>
</body>
</html>
```

The output will be:

Transitions

Transitions provide us with a way of changing a CSS property within a specified period of time. A good example is when changing the background color on mouse hover. With CCS3, you can easily animate from an old feature to a new feature within a specified duration. Consider the following example in which we animate the background color of a button on mouse hover:

```html
<!DOCTYPE html>
<html lang="en">
<head>
<meta charset="UTF-8">
<title>CSS3 Transition Feature</title>
<style type="text/css">
  button {
    color: #fff;
    border: none;
    padding: 10px 20px;
    font: bold 18px sans-serif;
    background: #1cc16e;
    -webkit-transition: background 2s; /* Safari 3.0 to 6.0 */
    transition: background 2s; /* modern browsers */
  }
  button:hover {
    background: #cc7c2b;
  }
</style>
</head>
<body>
  <button type="button"> Hover Mouse Cursor Here </button>
</body>
</html>
```

Animations

This is a CSS3 feature which takes the transitions feature a step further. When creating animations in CSS3, you should begin by setting the keyframes and naming an animation with keyframes declaration. Next, you should reference the keyframes by name via the *animation-name* property then add the *animation-duration* as well as other properties in order the animation behavior.

Consider the following that shows how a <div> box can be animated from one place to another:

```
<!DOCTYPE html>
<html lang="en">
<head>
<meta charset="UTF-8">
<title>CSS3 Translate Animation</title>
<style type="text/css">
  .box {
            margin: 50px;
    width:153px;
    height:103px;
    background:
url("/downloads/images/image1.png") no-repeat;
    position: relative;
    /* Chrome, Opera, Safari */
    -webkit-animation-name: moveit;
    -webkit-animation-duration: 2s;
    /* Standard syntax */
    animation-name: moveit;
    animation-duration: 2s;
  }
```

```
/* Chrome, Opera, Safari */
@-webkit-keyframes moveit {
  from {left: 0;}
  to {left: 50%;}
}

/* Standard syntax */
@keyframes moveit {
  from {left: 0;}
  to {left: 50%;}
}
</style>
</head>
<body>
  <p><strong>Animation:</strong> Ensure you have
specified the correct path to your image</p>
  <div class="box"></div>
</body>
</html>
```

Media Queries

With media queries in CSS3, you are able to format your documents so that they can appear well on devices with different screen sizes. In short, with media queries, you can create responsive web pages, which are web pages that scale well on devices with different screens such as mobile phones, tablets, desktop computers and laptops. Media queries depend on the screen size of the device in question. Consider the example given below:

```
<!DOCTYPE html>
<html lang="en">
<head>
<meta charset="UTF-8">
<title>Media Queries</title>
<style type="text/css">
  /* Smartphones (both portrait and landscape)*/
  @media screen and (min-width: 320px) and (max-width: 480px){
    body{
              background: #6ce6e1;
          }
  }
  /* Smartphones (portrait)*/
  @media screen and (max-width: 320px){
    body{
              background: #ccd280;
          }
  }
  /* Smartphones (landscape)*/
  @media screen and (min-width: 321px){
    body{
              background: #8cdfbb;
```

```css
            }
        }
        /* tablets, iPads (both portrait and landscape) */
        @media screen and (min-width: 768px) and (max-
    width: 1024px){
            body{
                            background: #ccb497;
                        }
        }
        /* tablets, iPads (portrait)*/
        @media screen and (min-width: 768px){
            body{
                            background: #c0e68c;
                        }
        }
        /* tablets, iPads (landscape)*/
        @media screen and (min-width: 1024px){
            body{
                            background: #c6b3f4;
                        }
        }
        /* Desktops and laptops*/
        @media screen and (min-width: 1224px){
            body{
                            background: #c6ff9d;
                        }
        }
        /* Large screens */
        @media screen and (min-width: 1824px){
            body{
                            background: #ddc0cb;
                        }
        }
    </style>
```

```
</head>
<body>
  <h1>CSS3 Media Queries</h1>

  <p>We have set the background to be different for
different devices based on their screen sizes.</p>

  <p><strong>Alternative:</strong> To see the
effect, open this in a different window trhen reset its
size. See changes in the background color.</p>

</body>
</html>
```

Just view the output of the above code in a new window then try to vary the size of the browser window. You will see the background color change based on the size of the screen.

Changing Column Width

You can use the device width or viewport size to change how content is displayed on the screen. In the following example, if viewport width of less than 768px, 100% of the viewport width will be covered, while if it's greater than 768px but less than 1024px, 750px will be covered:

```
<!DOCTYPE html>
<html lang="en">
<head>
<meta charset="UTF-8">
<title> Change Element's Width Via CSS Media
Queries</title>
<style type="text/css">
.container {
```

```css
      margin: 0 auto;
    background: #dbceff;
    box-sizing: border-box;
}
/* Mobile phones (both portrait and landscape) --------
-- */
@media screen and (max-width: 767px){
    .container {
      width: 100%;
      padding: 5px 10px;
    }
}


/* Tablets and iPads (both portrait and landscape) ----
------ */

@media screen and (min-width: 768px) and (max-
width: 1023px){

    .container {
      width: 750px;
      padding: 5px 10px;
    }
}
/* Desktops and laptops with low resolution */
@media screen and (min-width: 1024px) {
    .container {
      width: 980px;
      padding: 5px 15px;
    }
}
/* Desktops and laptops with high resolution */
@media screen and (min-width: 1280px) {
    .container {
```

```
    width: 1200px;
    padding: 5px 20px;
  }
}
</style>
</head>
<body>
    <div class="container">

        <p>You can use the device width or
viewport size to change how content is displayed on
the screen.</p>

        <p>You can use the device width or
viewport size to change how content is displayed on
the screen.</p>

    </div>
</body>
</html>
```

The display will be different based on the screen of the device in use.

Conclusion

This marks the end of this book. HTML5 is the latest version of HTML (Hyper Text Markup Language) while CSS3 is the latest version of CSS (Cascading Style Sheet). The two have introduced new features that you can take advantage of to develop a good-looking website. For instance, with HTML5, you don't need JavaScript for validation of your forms. With CSS3, you can create responsive web pages that scale well based on the size of the screen of the device under use.

www.ingramcontent.com/pod-product-compliance
Lightning Source LLC
Chambersburg PA
CBHW061032050326
40689CB00012B/2788